Leadership Mosaic
Putting the Pieces Together

Danny Valenzuela
Associate Certified Coach

TransitionExecs

August 2015

ACKNOWLEDGMENTS

This book would not have been possible without the support and encouragement of many people who have stood by me and used their leadership skills to inspire and motivate me.

My wife, Becky, who is always supportive of where my next venture will lead us and always has an encouraging word.

My mastermind group members Steve Broe, Will Jones, and Dan Robertson. They are always there to listen and provide me with their sincere feedback and thoughts.

My newsletter editor, Angela Rose, whose expertise and skills helped my words make sense.

My friends at the Arizona Chapter of the National Speakers Association, who encouraged me to write my first book and now my second.

My clients, who have allowed me to be a part of their lives and have taught me and helped me more than they can ever know.

CONTENTS

Are You Flexible in The Method You Use to Handle Conflict?

Conflict is inevitable, that's the bad news. The good news is that no meaningful change can take place without it, making it a powerful motivator for change. Therefore, it is important for us to learn the basics of conflict so when we face it, we can make it constructive instead of destructive.

We all have goals and expectations that define our personal agendas. When our agenda is the most important, we can tend to become very assertive. Other times, when it is not as important, we have no problem backing off or not pursuing it, or pursuing it less aggressively.

There are also different ways to deal with conflict. Knowing when to use each one is important. The Thomas-Kilmann Conflict Mode Instrument (TKI), defines five ways we handle conflict. It measures the relative frequency with which we use the five modes, which are:

> Competing – (My way or the highway)
> Collaborating – (The uniter)
> Compromising – (Let's make a deal)
> Avoiding – (I'll think about it tomorrow)
> Accommodating – (I'll go along to get along)

Each has its strengths and weaknesses. When we manage each one well, we can effectively manage conflict. We can't always say, "We're doing it my way," which is the *competing* mode. Sometimes we have to back off and use a different behavior. Flexibility should be our goal, so we can learn when and how to use each style appropriately.

The challenge is that most of us get good at or favor one or two styles, and tend to use them or rely on them in all circumstances. Much of this is learned when we are children. Therefore, it is important that we develop skills in all of the styles, to be able to use the one that is appropriate and most effective in a given situation.

Making good choices begins with understanding each style's strength, and being aware of its limits. We should display and respect each style, in order to maintain healthy and successful human relationships.

The key is not only to learn our own method of handling conflict, but to improve on how to read the key attributes of a conflict situation; how to choose and enact different conflict modes, and to learn how to engender more trust and supportive communication in both our personal and work life.

It is important to learn which conflict mode we might be using too much, usually out of habit, and which ones we might be using too little.

Why Do You Behave the Way You Do?

When we are born, we possess the essence of who we are, and as life happens, we find a way to relate to it. Early in life, we learned to feel safe and to cope with family situations and personal circumstances. We did this by developing a strategy based on natural talents and abilities.

We are born with a dominant type, and this orientation largely determines the ways in which we adapt to our early childhood development. By the time we are four or five years old, our consciousness has developed sufficiently to produce a separate sense of self. While still very fluid at this age, we begin to establish ourselves and find ways of fitting into our world.

One tool we can use to discover personality type is the Enneagram (pronounced ANY-a-gram). Its name comes from the Greek words for "nine" – enna – and "figure" – grammos, thus the nine-pointed figure. The Enneagram has been around for more than 2500 years. It is a geometric figure that defines the nine fundamental types of human nature and their complex interrelationships. It helps us recognize and understand an overall pattern in human behavior and underlying attitudes—including what attracts our attention. This tool explains why we behave the way we do, and points to specific directions for individual types and patterns of thinking, feeling, and acting.

Each point in the Enneagram can be seen as a set of personality types, with each number denoting one type. All personality types are equal, and studies have found that we possess some of each. However, one type is dominant in us and forms our personality and our social persona, which is how we meet the challenges of love and work. While each has different capacities, each also has different limitations.

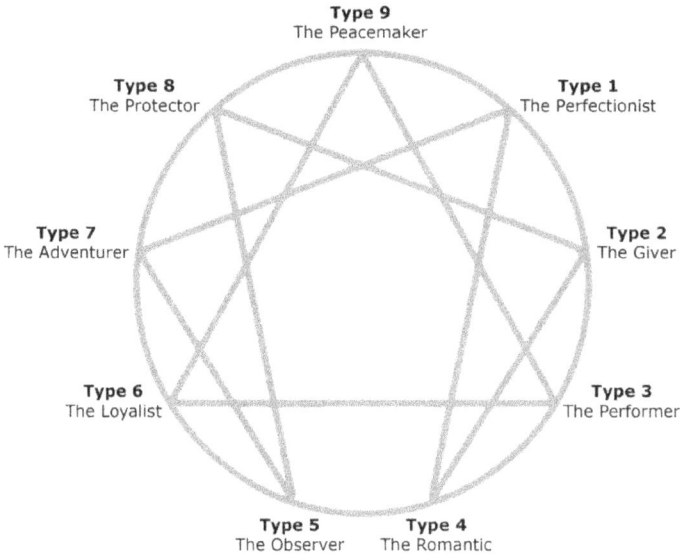

Type 9
The Peacemaker

Type 8
The Protector

Type 1
The Perfectionist

Type 7
The Adventurer

Type 2
The Giver

Type 6
The Loyalist

Type 3
The Performer

Type 5
The Observer

Type 4
The Romantic

1. Perfectionist, Reformer
2. Giver, Helper
3. Achiever, Performer, Producer
4. Romantic, Individualist, Connoisseur
5. Observer, Instigator, Sage
6. Doubter, Devil's advocate, Loyalist, Guardian.
7. Dreamer, Enthusiast, Visionary, Generalist
8. Leader, Boss, Top Dog, Challenger, Confronter
9. Diplomat, Mediator, Peacemaker, Preservationist

When you think of your personality type, which of the nine roles fits you best most of the time? Or, which of the word clusters comes closest?

So how can the Enneagram be of value? Being aware of the different types will give you a better understanding of others. It can give you a sense of compassion because you will recognize aspects of their particular habits and reaction in yourself. When we know our type, we can "catch ourselves in the act" as we move through the day. Once we have this self-awareness we can avoid reacting in negative ways.

As a source of self-knowledge, the Enneagram acts as a kind of "mirror," revealing features of our personality that are normally invisible to us. Most of the time, we function "out of habit" as if on automatic pilot, acting according to our basic personality type. When we can clearly see our habitual patterns, understanding what we do and why, we hold the key to getting out of the box—to freeing ourselves.

The Enneagram is a valuable tool coaches can use with individual clients and teams, helping them understand why they behave the way they do. In an organization or business, this can help in employee development, hiring decisions, or forming highly functional teams. If your team members are all type Nine *the mediator*, they may become stuck in neutral while they all try to mediate and negotiate. On the other hand, if they are all type Five *the observer*, there may be very little participation—making it difficult to extract knowledge or new ideas. Having a team or group of employees who are all the same type can be detrimental to your organization's effectiveness.

Some workplace applications of the Enneagram include:

> ➢ Personal development

- ➢ Executive coaching
- ➢ Leadership skill development
- ➢ Stress reduction and mediation
- ➢ Team building
- ➢ Project management
- ➢ Supervision
- ➢ Building workplace culture
- ➢ Motivation

None of the personality types is better or worse than any other. All types have unique assets and liabilities, strengths and weaknesses. You have all nine types in you. While it is common to find a little of ourselves in each of the nine types, one of them typically stands out as being closest to ourselves. This is our basic personality type.

Do You Think the World Is Imperfect And Needs Improvement?

Our Ascending Leader's Program™ uses the Enneagram as a tool to discuss personality types and ways to use this knowledge to enhance our behaviors and those of our team members. Self-knowledge helps us understand why we do things the way we do. It also helps us understand why others do things the way they do.

In this and subsequent newsletters I will discuss a particular personality type, how to recognize it, how we behave if it is our dominant type, and how to interact with others who fit this particular type.

In this issue, I will discuss personality Type 1, **The Reformer.** The Reformer is the Rational, Idealistic Type: Principled, Purposeful, Self-Controlled, and Perfectionistic. Reformers have a strong sense of right and wrong and are ethical and conscientious. They are well organized and have high standards, which can make them critical perfectionists.

It is easy to recognize a Reformer. They are neat and proper, sometimes meticulous, with a rigid posture and stiff upper lip. They may also present an overly pleasant demeanor. Reformers tend to think the world is imperfect, so they must work towards its improvement. They can be very critical of themselves, and when they get frustrated, they usually maintain a pleasant demeanor.

The average Reformer feels that others are indifferent to his or her principles and tries to convince them of the rightness of their viewpoint. A healthy Type 1 can approach life emotionally and possesses a strong sense of purpose and conviction. An unhealthy Type 1 can be close-minded and become uncompromising, bitter, or highly self-righteous.

The communication style of a Reformer is moralizing, teaching, preaching, judging, lecturing, and correcting. They excel in roles that require special attention to detail and can have an impact in an area where improvement is needed.

To get along with a Type 1, it is best to acknowledge their achievements, reassure them, and tell them you value their advice. It can also be a good idea to encourage them to lighten up and laugh at themselves. You may want to appeal to their sense of duty and ethics, be neat, well prepared, and organized, be on time, and stay on schedule. Instead of disagreeing with them, speak respectfully and ask "what if..." questions.

Of the three Centers of Intelligence (heart, head, and body), Reformers are in the body center, meaning they filter the world through an intelligence of kinesthetic and physical sensations along with gut instinct.

If you are a Type 1, or know one, understand that they normally hold their angry feelings in check. They hold their anger in their bodies and can become extremely tense and rigid with the effort to control themselves.

Suggestions and exercises for Type 1 team members are those that are self-nurturing.

- Spend time each day doing recreational activities

- Accentuate the importance of humor in your life
- Practice stress reduction, meditation, or yoga
- Take vacations to get away from work and compulsive actions

Remember, none of the personality types is better or worse than any other. All types have unique assets and liabilities, strengths and weaknesses. While it is common to find a little of ourselves in each of the nine types, one of them typically stands out as being closest to ourselves. This is our basic personality type.

Are You Meddling or Just Trying to be Helpful?

This is the second in a series of articles based on the nine personalities of the Enneagram. We use the Enneagram Personality Assessment in our Ascending Leader's Program™ to gain knowledge about our behaviors and those of our team members. Self-knowledge helps us understand why we do things the way we do. It also helps us understand why others do things the way they do.

In this issue, I will discuss personality Type 2, **The Helper.** The Helper is the Caring, Interpersonal Type: Demonstrative, Generous, People-Pleasing, and Possessive. Helpers are primarily motivated by the desire to meet the needs of others. They take pride in being needed by the team, and in helping make others successful. They are the most people-oriented of the Enneagram types, focusing on relationships and feeling best about themselves when they are meaningfully engaging with others.

Of the three Centers of Intelligence (heart, head, and body), Helpers are in the Emotional Center. This is the home of feeling based types that emphasize the heart for positive and negative feelings, empathy, and concern for others.

Famous Helpers include Gloria Estefan, Bill Cosby, and Sally Field. They rarely ask for assistance directly but appreciate when help is spontaneously offered. At the same time, they are not usually aware of the degree to which they give to others in order to gain appreciation, approval, and a feeling of being valued in return.

How can we recognize a Type 2? They focus more on

the feelings and needs of others than on themselves. They become sad when feeling unappreciated, unwanted, or unvalued. They focus on relationships, want to share the good in their lives, and enjoy supporting others with attention and care.

The average Helper can begin to fear that whatever they have been doing is not enough. They try to win people over and cultivate friendships by pleasing, flattering, and supporting them. Essentially, they are people pleasing. Many times they will say things like, "Let me do that for you," "Come get a hug," or "I won't take no for an answer."

An unhealthy Type 2 can be self-deceptive, with the tendency to become overly involved in the lives of others. They tend to manipulate others to get their own emotional needs met. Helpers find it hard to say no. They tend to feel drained and burned out because they overdo for others. In the workplace, they can be surprisingly angry and aggressive, acting as if they have no needs.

The Type 2 communicates by complimenting, being nice, sympathetic, giving advice, and sometimes being militant for a cause. They excel in roles that involve helping people, such as counselors, teachers, and health workers. They can also be found as actresses, actors, and motivational speakers. They work in areas that help others, such as receptionists, secretaries, assistants, and clothing consultants.

Coaching a Helper may focus on their strengths, which are being empathic, supportive, motivating, and warm. For development purposes, coaches assist Helpers with understanding how they accommodate others, their indirectness, feeling unappreciated, and tendency to overextend themselves.

If you are a Type 2, or know one, know that they like to be appreciated. Be specific and take an interest in their problems, though they will probably try to focus on yours. Let them know that they are important and special to you, and be gentle if you decide to criticize them.

Suggestions and exercises for Helpers are about building self-esteem.

- Engage in activities that give pleasure and satisfaction but do not involve being with others.
- Reparent your inner child by talking to yourself in nurturing and loving ways, as you would a child, but stay in parent stance.
- Give yourself some of the attention and pampering you usually give others.
- Value the love that is in your life instead of focusing on what is missing.

Remember, none of the personality types is better or worse than any other. All types have unique assets and liabilities, strengths and weaknesses. While it is common to find a little of ourselves in each of the nine types, one of them typically stands out as being closest to ourselves. This is our basic personality type.

Do You Engage Only in Activities You Are Good at in Order to Avoid Failure?

This is the third in a series of articles based on the nine personalities of the Enneagram. We use the Enneagram Personality Assessment in our Coaching and Ascending Leader's Program™ to gain knowledge about our behaviors and those of our team members. Self-knowledge helps us understand why we do things the way we do. It also helps us understand why others do things the way they do.

In this issue, I will discuss personality Type 3, **The Achiever.** The Achiever is a motivator, a status seeker and one who is driven and image conscious. Achievers feel the need to succeed, and they are energetic, optimistic, and self-assured. They are primarily motivated by their desire to achieve a successful image, and they feel it's more important to get something done than to get it right. While poised and diplomatic, Achievers can be overly concerned with image and the opinion of others.

Threes can be challenged by competitiveness and workaholism. They want others to see them as successful. As such, Achievers exemplify the human need for attention, encouragement, and affirmation. They engage in competition because they fear being overshadowed by someone else.

Threes use their Heart Center to focus on how others respond to them in terms of gaining their respect and admiration. These Achievers read their audience quite well and can change their persona in order to elicit the response they desire. Because of this, they are called the "chameleons" of the Enneagram.

Famous Achievers include Michael Jordan, Bill Clinton, Denzel Washington, Sharon Stone, George Clooney, Demi Moore, Halle Berry, and Vince Lombardi. They figure out practical ways to use their resources, communicate by talking about results, work under pressure to achieve the outcomes they want, and pursue their goals until they attain them.

How do we recognize a Type 3? They exemplify a desire to be their best self, to develop all of their potential, and to value others and themselves. They have a generous smile as well as a pleasantly seductive demeanor. They make you feel appreciated, fully heard, and good about yourself. Threes are the "stars" of the personality types – people of tremendous drive, ambition, and belief in themselves.

The average Achiever is well intentioned, an excellent communicator, motivator, and promoter. They can be very effective in building morale and company spirit. They value excellence and accomplishment, and enjoy helping others discover how to shine. This makes them feel real, and they impress others with their sincerity. At their best they are tender, genuine, and affectionate – role models and heroes who inspire others.

Unhealthy Achievers can drive themselves too hard, leading to unnecessary stress. This can cause them to go on "autopilot," or attempt to get thru difficulties without being bothered. As a result, they lose focus and involve themselves in busy work to give the appearance that they are getting things done. Sometimes they become stubborn and refuse help, not wanting to accept that they have a problem. The Type 3 communicates by enthusiastically motivating themselves and others for success. They are frequently in management or leadership positions in business, law, banking, the computer field, and politics. They also tend to be in the public eye as broadcasters and performers.

Coaching an Achiever may focus on their strengths, which are energetic, entrepreneurial, confident, and results oriented. For development purposes, coaches assist Achievers by helping them understand the extent to which they over identify with their work as well as the personal price they pay for doing so. They expect a clear discussion and a firm decision about their coaching goals early in the coaching process. A key motivator for development is to have them see themselves as successful without feeling the pressure of always having to prove it.

If you are a Type 3, or know one, know that they are in their element when they drive for results. They have the ability to maintain a laser like focus. The core of their Enneagram personality architecture is to achieve outstanding goals and results.

Suggestions and exercises for Achievers are about relaxation and self-nurturing.

- Schedule time every day to rest and practice meditation or stress-reduction techniques including massages, steam baths, or saunas.
- Make time for activities you value outside of work.
- Reduce stress by appreciating and accepting your present level of success.
- Take a vacation and leave all your work at home.

Remember, none of the personality types is better or worse

than any other. All types have unique assets and liabilities, strengths and weaknesses. While it is common to find a little of ourselves in each of the nine types, one of them typically stands out as being closest to ourselves. This is our basic personality type.

Are You Seen as Difficult and Contradictory – and You Like that About Yourself?

This is the fourth in a series of articles based on the nine personalities of the Enneagram. We use the Enneagram Personality Assessment in our Coaching and Ascending Leader's Program™. The Enneagram helps us gain self-knowledge and self-awareness. It acts as a *mirror* to reveal aspects of our personality that are not normally visible to us.

This issue focuses on personality Type 4, **The Individualist.** Individualists are motivated by the need to experience their feelings, to be understood, to search for the meaning of life, and to avoid being ordinary. They are also driven by the desire to express their individuality.

One of the biggest challenges Individualists face is learning to let go of feelings from the past; they tend to nurse wounds and hold on to negative feelings about those who have hurt them.

Fours are from the Heart Center of the triad of our ego self. They are the most sensitive of all the Enneagram styles, although their sensitivity is generally focused on their own internal reactions and feelings. They are primarily concerned with the development of self-image.

Famous Individualists include John McEnroe, Barbara Streisand, Angelina Jolie, James Dean, Julio Iglesias, Carlos Santana, and Johnny Depp. They are concerned about the feelings of others and dislike doing the same ordinary things repeatedly.

How do we identify a Type 4? They engage in

extensive introspection; they want to be unique or special; they can appear moody; they use self-referencing language and want to be understood. Fours typically have problems with negative self-image and low self-esteem.

The average Individualist is artistic and imaginative, fantasizing, introverted, self-absorbed, self-conscious, self-indulgent, and self-pitying. They worry that others will not appreciate them for their uniqueness. They feel they are missing out on life and exempt themselves from "the rules," becoming sensual, pretentious, and unproductive.

Unhealthy Individualists can be self-destructive, alienated, and emotionally self-tormenting. They fear they are wasting their lives. Their repressed rage results in depression, apathy, and constant fatigue.

Healthy Individualists are inspiring, creative, and express the universal human condition. They are also self-aware, intuitive, and individualistic. Their basic desire is to find themselves and discover their significance. They focus on their own feelings and preferences to create a clear sense of personal identity. They are eloquent and subtle, exploring their feelings and finding ways to share them with others.

The Individualist's communication style is melancholic, idealistic, emotional, and dramatic. They are typically employed as visual or performing artists, entrepreneurs, and interior or fashion designers.

When coaching an Individualist it is important to remember that their reactions to feedback can vary. Negative feedback may cause them to feel defective. They prefer a coach who is sympathetic, understanding, and warm. Being objective and direct will help them the most.

If you know a Type 4, give plenty of compliments and be a supportive friend or partner. Help them love and value themselves. Respect them for their gifts of intuition and vision, and don't tell them they are overreacting or too sensitive.

Suggestions and exercises for Individualists are about self-esteem.

- Be proud of your special gifts, talents, and accomplishments.
- Find ways to make everyday duties and responsibilities creative and playful.
- Commit yourself to creative work the will bring out your best.
- If it is not possible to work in a creative career, take the time to germinate your ideas in your off-work hours.

Remember, none of the personality types is better or worse than any other. All types have unique assets and liabilities, strengths and weaknesses. While it is common to find a little of ourselves in each of the nine types, one of them typically stands out as being closest to ourselves. This is our basic personality type.

How Do You Communicate With the Intellectual, Innovative, Quiet Type?

This is the fifth in a series of articles based on the nine personalities of the Enneagram. We use the Enneagram Personality Assessment in our Coaching and Ascending Leader's Program™. The Enneagram helps us gain self-knowledge and self-awareness. It acts as a mirror to reveal aspects of our personality that are not normally visible to us. We create certain prototypes in our minds and then fit into them.

Personality theorists make two kinds of statements. One describes the things we all have in common and are inherent in human beings.

The other is that the differences among people are generally learned, rather than generic. In essence, there is only one of us.

Somewhere in between what we have in common with everyone else and what we share with no one else are some characteristics that overlap with some people but not with others.

This issue focuses on personality Type 5, **The Investigator.** Investigators thirst for knowledge and use emotional detachment as a way of keeping involvement with others to a minimum. They tend to be introverted, needing time alone for reading and thinking.

Investigators often fear that their skills are insufficient and they need to prepare more before they take their place in the world. Their worry that the needs of others will distract them from their own projects leads them to shut out intrusions. They spend much of their time alone studying, practicing, and acquiring more knowledge, resources, and skills.

Fives are in the Thinking Triad, which focuses on finding a sense of inner guidance and support. In some spiritual traditions, they are called the *quiet mind*. However, we seldom have access to this peaceful, spacious quality of the mind. For most of us, the mind is a chatterbox. That's why some people spend years in monasteries or at retreats trying to quiet their minds. Investigators respond by retreating from life and reducing their personal needs.

Famous Investigators include Albert Einstein, Bill Gates, Thomas Edison, Bobby Fischer, Stephen King, and Robert DeNiro. They are good at analyzing problems, prefer silence in order to concentrate, and are quite satisfied with working by themselves.

How do we identify a Type 5? To them everything is potential knowledge. They intellectualize feelings, are emotionally detached, pursue information and knowledge, and are usually the calm ones in a crisis. However, they can become easily drained.

The average Investigator is overly intellectual, endlessly analytically, detached and preoccupied. They feel unsure of themselves, thus preferring the safety of their minds. They study, practice, and collect knowledge.

Unhealthy Investigators are reclusive, isolated, and cynical. To gain security they cut off all connections with the world, rejecting all but basic needs.

Healthy Investigators are experts, ingenious, perceptive, and knowledgeable. When they become capable and competent to live in the world, they become clear-minded, profound, and compassionate. As thinkers, they can become very original, inventive, and artful.

The Investigator's communication style is to explain, systematize, and analyze. They are typically employed as scientists, engineers, writers, hi-tech specialists, mathematicians, and inventors.

When coaching an Investigator, it is important to remember that they tend to compartmentalize information they receive. They hear one piece of data, place it in a category in their minds, and then move on to other data without seeing the connection between the pieces of information. They don't like to be asked questions about their feelings unless they are very familiar with their coach.

If you know a Type 5, speak to them in a straightforward and brief manner. Give them time to process feeling and thoughts. If they seem aloof, distant, or arrogant, it may be because they are feeling uncomfortable. Don't come at them like a bulldozer. Help them avoid big gatherings, other people's loud music, and intrusions on their privacy.

Suggestions and exercises for Investigators are about getting out of their head and into doing.
- Don't avoid conflict, take risks, and speak up.
- Become more active by taking up creative or sports activities.
- Value being in the present.
- Become a member of a group where it is acceptable to speak or not to speak.

If you're a Type 5, make sure you say positive things

about yourself. You will experience being an individual fully when you empty yourself of preconceived ideas and categories. Finally, you don't have to be the smartest person.

Remember, none of the personality types is better or worse than any other. All types have unique assets and liabilities, strengths and weaknesses. While it is common to find a little of ourselves in each of the nine types, one of them typically stands out as being closest to ourselves. This is our basic personality type.

Before You Act, Do You Focus On What Can Go Wrong?

This is the sixth in a series of articles based on the nine personalities of the Enneagram. We use the Enneagram Personality Assessment in our Coaching and Ascending Leader's Program™ to gain self-knowledge and self-awareness. It acts as a mirror to reveal aspects of our personality that are not normally visible to us.

Personality theorists make two kinds of statements. One describes the things we all have in common, traits that are inherent in all human beings.

The other states that the differences among people are generally learned, rather than generic. In essence, there is only one of each of us.

Somewhere in between what we have in common with everyone else and what we share with no one else are characteristics that overlap with some people but not with others.

This issue focuses on personality Type 6, **The Loyalist.** Loyalists are motivated by their desire to alleviate risk. They are also tenacious in their loyalty, defenders of their faith, and protectors of their traditions. Sixes are the most loyal to their friends and to their beliefs, as well as to ideas and systems.

Loyalists have insightful minds and are prone to worry, often creating worst-case scenarios. This helps them feel prepared in case something goes wrong. Some Loyalists are overly fearful, while others move toward fear as a way of proving they have no fear.

Sixes are in the Head Triad; they are called the doubting mind. When considering what to do, how to solve a problem, and what decisions to make, they immediately conjecture "*What if this happened,*" "*What if that doesn't work,*" and more. They need to consider what can go wrong before they commit to a course of action.

Famous Loyalists include Julia Roberts, Matt Damon, Howard Cossell, Steve Martin, Michelle Pfeiffer, Tom Hanks, Malcolm X, and Ted Turner. When Sixes give their word about something, they keep it.

How do we identify a Type 6? They appear worried, suspicious, aggressively self-protective, warm and likeable, strong and fearless. They have searching eyes, are sharply attentive and skeptical. They can make you feel distrusted, cross-examined, awkward, trusted, warm, part of the team, misled, and uncertain.

Some proverbs that identify a Type Six include: *United we stand, divided we fall. Readiness is all. Two heads are better than one. Better safe than sorry*.

The average Loyalist is obedient, a traditionalist, dependent, hesitant, defensive, and rebellious. They begin to fear they will lose their independence but also believe they need more support. They worry they cannot meet the demands placed on them so they try to resist having more pressure put upon them.

Unhealthy Loyalists are insecure, clingingly dependent, overreacting, and can be hysterical and irrational, feeling their actions may have harmed their own security.

Healthy Loyalists are self-affirming, courageous, emotionally engaged, and loyal. They let go of the belief that they must rely on someone or something outside themselves for support. They reinforce their self-image by working to create and sustain mutually beneficial systems.

The Loyalist's communication style is questioning, cautioning, doubting, and challenging.

When coaching a Loyalist it's important to remember that they become especially anxious when they are about to receive feedback. They like to discuss their coaching goals, recognizing that doing so provides them and their coach with a common direction. Because they are prone to self-doubt and second-guessing themselves, they may revise and revisit their coaching goals multiple times during the first few coaching sessions.

If you know a Type 6, be direct, clear, and listen to them carefully. Work things through with them, and reassure them that everything is OK. Push them gently toward new experiences and try not to overreact to their overreacting.

Suggestions and exercises for Loyalists are about self-confidence.

- Try to be around people who are accepting, trustworthy, and encouraging.
- Notice and accept the positive things people say about you.
- Remember that there is no one "right" way to live, as long as you are satisfied with what you are doing.
- Remember it is OK to make mistakes.

Remember, none of the personality types is better or worse than any other. All types have unique assets and liabilities, strengths and weaknesses. While it is common to find a little of ourselves in each of the nine types, one of them typically stands out as being closest to ourselves. This is our basic personality type.

Do You Lighten Up Unhappy People and Get Them to See the Bright Side?

This is the seventh in a series of articles based on the nine personalities of the Enneagram. We use the Enneagram Personality Assessment in our Coaching and Ascending Leader's Program™ to gain self-knowledge and self-awareness. It acts as a mirror to reveal aspects of our personality that are not normally visible to us.

Personality theorists make two kinds of statements. One describes the things we all have in common, traits that are inherent in all human beings.

The other states that the differences among people are generally learned, rather than generic. In essence, there is only one of each of us.

Somewhere in between what we have in common with everyone else and what we share with no one else are characteristics that overlap with some people but not with others.

This issue focuses on Enneagram personality Type 7, **The Enthusiast.** Enthusiasts crave the stimulation of new ideas, people, and expectations. They also avoid pain and create elaborate plans for the future that allow them to keep all their options open.

Enthusiasts are adventurers, optimistic, spontaneous, versatile, and fun loving. They need to avoid pain and are energetic and embracing. Enthusiasts are motivated by the desire to see possibilities. They are eternal optimists and enjoy exploring new things beyond the status quo.

Sevens are in the Head Triad; they are called the synthesizing mind, responding instantaneously to stimulation, moving in a nanosecond to a new idea, then triggering another idea, and so forth. They enjoy learning and gathering information, but prefer to learn many different things. As a result, they have a breadth, but not necessarily a depth, of knowledge.

Because they constantly seek new and exciting experiences, they can become distracted and exhausted by staying on the go. They typically have problems with impatience and impulsiveness.

Famous Enthusiasts include Robin Williams, Jerry Seinfeld, Joan Rivers, Bette Midler, George Lopez, Jim Carrey, Catherine Zeta-Jones, and Eddie Murphy. They feel challenged when they have to stay focused on one thing for any length of time, becoming distracted by new thoughts and external stimuli.

How do we identify a Type 7? They have bright and happy eyes, love bright colors, have easy-going body movement, are charming, sharp-minded, mischievous, and aggressive but loveable. They bring craziness, eclectic connections, delight, adventure, impulsiveness, spontaneity, and energy to a group.

Some proverbs that identify a Six include: *Where there is no vision, the people perish. Nothing is wonderful when you get used to it. A rolling stone gathers no moss. Moderation is a fatal thing; nothing succeeds like excess.*

The average Enthusiast is extroverted, hyperactive, impulsive, materialistic, and excessive. They fear that they are missing out on other, more worthwhile experiences, thus become restless and interested in having more options available to them. They can be demanding, but are seldom satisfied when their demands are met.

Unhealthy Enthusiasts are insensitive towards others. They tend to be scattered, erratic, compulsive, panic-stricken, and hysterical. They are highly impulsive and irresponsible, doing whatever promises temporary relief from their anxiety.

Healthy Enthusiasts are appreciative, blissful, enthusiastic, grateful for blessings, accomplished and practical generalists. They let go of the belief that they require specific objects and experiences to be fulfilled. They fully engage in life.

The Enthusiast's communication style is talkative, storytelling, speculating, and brainstorming.

When coaching an Enthusiast it's important to remember that they can be excited about coaching, but will avoid coaching meetings if they anticipate feeling uncomfortable, inadequate, or restricted. Patience is required because Sevens may be late or miss their appointments so often that coaches can feel frustrated and even disrespected. In coaching sessions, they talk more than listen and want to discuss as much information as possible. They also like the idea of generating goals, but resist adhering to them.

If you know a Type 7, give them companionship, affection, and freedom. Appreciate their grand visions, listen to their stories, and engage them in stimulating conversation and laughter. Don't try to change their style, just accept them the way they are. Don't tell them what to do.

Suggestions and exercises for Enthusiasts are about health and stress.

- Cultivate healthy habits of eating, sleeping, and exercise. Some Sevens have the tendency to go to extremes and neglect their health.
- Take up an exercise program such as swimming or tai chi.
- Be careful not to eat, drink, or spend to excess when stressed.
- Remove your rose-colored glasses and take into account the dark or negative side of life for reality and balance.
- Accept feelings, trusting they will pass.
- Be tactful and sensitive, trying to see things from other's point of view.

Remember, none of the personality types is better or worse than any other. All types have unique assets and liabilities, strengths and weaknesses. While it is common to find a little of ourselves in each of the nine types, one of them typically stands out as being closest to ourselves. This is our basic personality type.

Are You Annoyed by Whiners but Protective of the Noble Weak?

This is the eighth in a series of articles based on the nine personalities of the Enneagram. We use the Enneagram Personality Assessment in our Coaching and Ascending Leader's Program™ to gain self-knowledge and self-awareness. It acts as a mirror to reveal aspects of our personality that are not normally visible to us.

Personality theorists make two kinds of statements. One describes the things we all have in common, traits that are inherent in all human beings.

The other states that the differences among people are generally learned, rather than generic. In essence, there is only one of each of us.

Somewhere in between what we have in common with everyone else and what we share with no one else are characteristics that overlap with some people but not with others.

This issue focuses on Enneagram personality Type 8,

The Challenger. Challengers enjoy taking on challenges themselves as well as giving others opportunities that challenge them to exceed in some way. Eights have enormous willpower and vitality, and they feel most alive when exercising these capacities in the world.

Challengers are leaders. They are the bosses and the confrontational power-seekers. They are assertive, direct, self-reliant, self-confident, and protective. Eights are primarily motivated by the desire to establish self-reliance.

Eights are in the Body Center Triad, meaning they filter the world through an intelligence of kinesthetic and physical sensations along with gut instinct. Body-based types lead with the body movement, sense awareness, gut-level feelings, personal security, and social belonging. Their focus is on taking control of themselves and their environment, and taking action in practical ways.

Eights are quick to anger and even quicker to respond. They experience anger as energy that can overtake them unless it can be released immediately. Once the anger is expressed, they tend to move on.

Expect an Eight to challenge you, to test your integrity, strength, or conviction. Don't try to dominate them and force decisions; this is their domain, and they will laugh your efforts away. Don't back down and be weak, either. They are annoyed by anyone they feel is a whiner or wimp, but will protect the noble weak.

Famous Challengers include Johnny Cochran, Robert Shapiro, Martin Luther King, Jr., General Norman Schwarzkopf, Frank Sinatra, Barbara Walters, Russell Crowe, and Sean Connery.

How do we identify a Type 8? They exemplify the desire to be independent and to take care of themselves. They are assertive and passionate about life, meeting it head on with self-confidence and strength. They are resourceful and stand up for themselves. They are people of vision and action, taking the initiative and making things happen, protecting the people in their lives while empowering others to stand on their own.

Some proverbs that identify an Eight include:

Damn the torpedoes, full speed ahead. If you don't like the heat, get out of the kitchen. Discretion is the better part of valor. No one tells me what to do.

Average Challengers are enterprising and industrious, dominating, confrontational, combative, and intimidating. They are people of vision and action. Honor is important to them because their word is their bond. Many times, they are full of bluster and bravado.

Unhealthy Challengers can be ruthless and cruel, extremely controlling, confrontational, and territorial. They sometimes throw their weight around in various ways, by swaggering, being willful, and bluffing.

Healthy Challengers are self-restrained, self-confident, and strong leaders. They are influential, having quick minds with visions for practical possibilities. They are often charismatic and able to attract the support of others to join in their vision. They are good at getting others to stretch their abilities and surpass their own expectations.

The Challenger's communication style is confronting, commanding, unmasking, controlling, threatening, and direct.

When coaching a Challenger it's important to remember that they are straightforward and do not like to be asked indirect questions, perceiving these as time wasting or manipulative. It is best to ask succinct, candid questions. Eights usually want to focus on the biggest picture possible, with details used as supportive information. They don't like to waste time and are prone to taking immediate action.

If you know a Type 8, stand up for yourself. Be confident, strong, and direct. Acknowledge their contributions but don't flatter them. If they speak to you in an assertive way, don't automatically think it's a personal attack. If they curse, scream, and stomp around, it's just the way they are.

Suggestions and exercises for Challengers are about relationships.

- Beware that when you are "direct" you may unintentionally intimidate others.
- Resist dismissing or invalidating other's experience or views.
- Express your appreciation aloud and often.
- Avoid driving others as hard as you drive yourself.
- Learn to negotiate
- Remember that sparring can be stimulating to an Eight but not to most other types.

Remember, none of the personality types is better or worse than any other. All types have unique assets and liabilities, strengths and weaknesses. While it is common to find a little of ourselves in each of the nine types, one of them typically stands out as being closest to ourselves. This is our basic personality type.

Do You Say What You Really Think or Always Try to Keep Things in Harmony?

This issue focuses on Enneagram personality Type 9, **The Peacemaker.** Peacemakers are the most basic or undistorted personality type. They have a problem with priorities and find it difficult to change directions or shift attention to what is most important.

Peacemakers are balanced, accepting, and harmonious. They find it difficult to face priorities or conflict. They tend to find union with others, mediating conflicts, avoiding tension, and keeping things in harmony. The value that Nines are attracted to is harmony. They relish calm, prize peace, and appreciate regularity.

Nines are in the Body Center Triad, meaning they filter the world through an intelligence of kinesthetic and physical sensations along with gut instinct. Body-based types lead with the body movement, sense awareness, gut-level feelings, personal security, and social belonging. Their focus is on taking control of themselves and their environment, and taking action in practical ways.

Nines are called the Peacemakers because no type is more devoted to the quest for internal and external peace for themselves and others. Nines can have the strength of Eights, the sense of fun and adventure of Sevens, the dutifulness of Sixes, the intellectualism of Fives, the creativity of Fours, the attractiveness of Threes, the generosity of Twos, and the idealism of Ones. However, they don't have a sense of their own identity.

Famous Peacemakers include Kevin Costner, Sophia Loren, Morgan Freeman, Coretta Scott King, Sylvester Stallone, Shaquille O'Neal, Joe Montana, Mahatma Gandhi, Dalai Lama, and Jimmy Smits.

How do we identify a Type 9? Nines appear easygoing, nonjudgmental, and diplomatic. They also show their support of others through affirming comments, head nodding, and saying "Uh-huh." However, this does not always mean they agree, just that they hear what others are saying.

Some proverbs that identify a Nine include:

Unity is strength. Moderation in all things. Don't rock the boat. Not to decide is to decide. Diplomacy is the peaceful substitute for shooting. Cooperation is spelled with two letters: we. The greatest strength is shown in standing still.

Average Peacemakers are accommodating, unassuming, passive, submissive, and philosophical. Competition is not appealing to them, nor is one right way, or pressure to choose. They need to know exactly what is expected of them and what their role is. Nines value relationships more than anything and will work towards collaboration.

Unhealthy Peacemakers can be neglectful, self-conscious, inadequate, disoriented, and self-abandoning. They can be too sensitive to criticism and critical of themselves for lacking initiative and discipline. Insecurities about their desire to please make it difficult to say no to people.
Healthy Peacemakers are self-sufficient, receptive, supportive, peacemaking, stable, and nurturing. They have the ability to be agreeable and to comfort others

with endurance and strength. They can mediate between people and lessen conflicts. They can be very effective in negotiations or human resource capacities.

The Peacemaker's communication style is monotonous, rambling, appeasing, and soothing. They have trouble getting to the point, being linear and controlled, or quite scattered.

When coaching a Peacemaker it's important to remember that they have to have a strong connection with a coach before they fully engage in the experience. This is particularly important when they are about to hear constructive feedback and feel stressed. They prefer specific details and multiple interpretations of the key issues, which mirrors the way they process information.

If you know a Type 9, understand that they like to listen and be of service, but not be taken advantage of. If they meander while speaking, listen until they finish. They like good discussions, but not confrontational ones. While you should give them time to finish things and make decisions, it's okay to nudge them gently and nonjudgmentally.

Suggestions and exercises for Peacemakers are about relationships and anger.

- Take the first step to change a situation that isn't right instead of hoping that things will change by themselves.
- Bring up your problems when talking with others rather than only listening to theirs.
- Tell people when you want to be alone.
- Learn to become aware of and then appropriately express your anger.

- Avoid acting as if everything is fine when it isn't.
- Learn to feel the buildup of anger in your body.

Remember, none of the personality types is better or worse than any other. All types have unique assets and liabilities, strengths and weaknesses. While it is common to find a little of ourselves in each of the nine types, one of them typically stands out as being closest to ourselves. This is our basic personality type.

Are You Living the Black Belt Mentality In Leadership?

In today's world, many individuals on a leadership track want instant gratification, instant rewards, instant feedback, instant stardom, instant career paths, and instant anointment as leaders. Yes, they want it now. Like the J. G. Wentworth commercial, "It's my money, and I want it now."

How long does it take to earn acknowledgement as a leader? I suspect some people reach that level of recognition faster than others do, yet all of us have to earn it. From time to time, I coach young managers and potential leaders who say, "I can be the CEO of this company." Sure, confidence is important, but developing the skills and talents to be an effective leader takes time. Many individuals do not want to make the effort to develop their leadership skills, develop their emotional maturity or credibility, or go through a process of growth and development to earn their Black Belt in leadership.

What does it take to earn a Black Belt in leadership? The same process as to earn a Black Belt in karate. It takes time, training, practice, emotional maturity and the right frame of mind. It's living the Black Belt Mentality.

The Black Belt Mentality is based on the following story. A young man asked his Master, "Master, when will I be a Black Belt?" And the Master replied, "You will never be a Black Belt. For anyone who would ask such a question doesn't have the patience, will, and discipline to do what is required to become a Black Belt."

Therefore, living the Black Belt Mentality requires that we walk with an open mind each day. It requires the desire to become a problem solver, to learn something new, and to pursue that practice with all our heart.

In Western culture, we have the belt system associated with martial arts, beginning with the White Belt and ending with the 10th Degree Black Belt Grand Master. To become a 10th Degree Black Belt Grand Master, one must practice more than 40 years.

Originally, in martial arts there was no belt system. You started with a white belt, and after years and years of training, the belt turned black because it was soiled and dirty from all the hard work. The true Black Belt wants to turn his belt back to white. The way to accomplish this is to keep training, working, and striving, until the fibers tear and fray to reveal the white cloth once again.

So how long does it take to become a leader? The answer is you can be one now, and continue to train, work, and strive to improve your skills. It is important to sustain that drive and embrace the Black Belt Mentality, and that is all about patience, will, and discipline. If you follow that formula, and practice it every day, you will develop your leadership skills and earn your leadership Black Belt, eventually being recognized as a 10th Degree Black Belt Grand Master in leadership.

Providing your valued employees the tools to become Black Belt Leaders is essential to helping them grow, stay centered, balanced, calm during a crisis, and creative and effective in everything they do. Someone once said, "Leadership is not about what you know; it's about what you are willing to learn."

Do You Use Humor as a Way of Being Serious?

Humor is a leadership competency, but many people in leadership positions are unskilled at it. They may be too serious, have problems telling a joke, don't know how to use humor appropriately, or maybe just appear humorless. Those who are skilled at using humor tend to have a good sense of humor, can laugh at themselves and with others, and use humor appropriately to ease tensions.

Leaders who learn not to take themselves too seriously and who use humor and humility are typically well balanced and self-confident. It keeps their ego in check and their feet on the ground.

Humor is an essential element of life and work. If we use it properly, it can defuse tension in a crisis. But there is a time and place for everything, and humor at the expense of others is inappropriate and harmful in the work environment.

There are many types of humor available to us. There is good humor and negative humor, constructive humor and destructive humor. We all know people who are humorous and we have, no doubt, heard humorous stories that are used to make a point.

We can learn to find humor in everyday situations; it's not simply about telling jokes. Humorous events in our everyday lives are a good source of stories. Think about a ridiculous situation you have experienced, funny kids, pets or hobbies. Then there is always the news or simply looking for humor around you.

It's important to keep humor in good taste. People are turned off by political, sexist, ethnic, and religious humor. It's also important to avoid race, gender, and culture when trying to be humorous. Don't make fun of others or make them feel or look bad.

Self-deprecating humor—poking fun at yourself—is usually safe and can lead to increased respect. Funny or embarrassing things that happened to you, your flaws, or mistakes you've made can add humor to a situation. It also makes you more human and endearing.

Never use humor as a shield or a defense technique, and choose the right time for using humor. Sometimes it's best to follow the lead of others, not being the first to use humor but being second or third until you find your funny bone. Until you get good or natural at it, you can improve your results by using a little exaggeration, being brief, and omitting unnecessary words.

Humor can be motivating. Not all leaders are the nicest people you would want to work for, but if they help you accomplish what you want, and have fun doing it, then it has been a far better place than if humor was absent.

To get better at humor, study the pros. Read How to Be Funny by Jon Macks and Laughing Matters by Joel Goodman. You can also go to comedy performances and observe how the professionals do it.

Humor is common in many forms of communication. It creates an open atmosphere by awakening positive emotions that enhance listening, understanding, and acceptance of messages.

Change. Why Is It So Difficult For So Many?

For some, change is readily accepted; for others, resistance is the norm.

At our annual conference last month, the leadership of the National Speakers Association announced a rebranding effort. The most visible aspect was the name change to "Platform." I am sure they spent a considerable amount of time and resources to develop the new brand, but the announcement certainly caught everyone by surprise.

For many it was a welcome change, but based on the emails and videos sent out from the leadership team almost immediately after the announcement, it appears that many of our members are resistant. Now it appears they must spend more time and effort to rethink their intentions and quell the uprising.

Organizations don't just change because systems change. Organizations change because people within them have made personal decisions to change. Only then can the organization reap the benefits of change. When dealing with people, the challenge is to help and support those within the organization. Change—even something as simple as a name change—can be traumatic, especially for long-term members who have grown up with the name and brand of the National Speakers Association.

An article in Mind Tools™ mentions the following four stages people typically go through as they adjust to change:
1. The initial reaction may be shock or denial as they react to a change from the status quo.

Once reality starts to hit, they tend to react negatively and move to the second stage.

2. They may feel angry, fear the impact, and actively resist or protest the change. Some wrongly fear negative consequences or identify threats to their position. At this stage the organization may experience disruption, which can easily spiral into chaos.
3. Then people stop focusing on what they lost. They start to let go and accept the change. They accept what is good and not so good and learn to adapt.
4. In the final stage they accept the change and can start to embrace it.

Once people get to the final stage, the organization can start to reap the benefits. I suspect the National Speakers Association is in the process of getting members from Stage 1 to Stage 2. The turning point is Stage 3, when it will come out of the danger zone. I am sure they will be successful in minimizing the impact and help people adapt more quickly. Getting members through this transition is critical. Something as simple as an Impact Analysis may have given more insight as to the consequences of the decision.

We have to be aware that the world changes; we have to change as well. As the pace of change continues to increase, an organization's change capability will become a greater requirement for sustainable performance.

Organizations that have stayed stagnant and resisted change are no longer with us; they typically die a slow death. Organizations that are investing in change capabilities are more likely to capitalize on future opportunities. Is your organization one of them?

What is Important to You and How Would You Like to Be?

Now that Thanksgiving is over, many of us turn our focus to the Christmas holidays. During the holiday season, we tend to take more time to relax and enjoy our family or those important to us. Perhaps we took a four-day weekend for Thanksgiving and are looking forward to four-day weekends for Christmas and New Year's as well.

Many individuals find it easy to take time off during holidays but difficult to relax and enjoy personal leisure other times of the year. What makes it so difficult to discipline ourselves to enjoy a little more balance during every season? After all, isn't work-life balance important to us, and doesn't it help us be what we would like to be?

In theory, work-life balance seems to make sense – splitting our time with our work life and also enjoying personal activities and leisure time. But "work-life balance," as we traditionally think about it, may not actually exist. Because technology has redefined our leisure time, this is truer today than in the past.

As organizations embrace workforce mobility, opportunities for innovation and communication between team members increase. These increased opportunities to work from home or remotely with colleagues and coworkers causes an overlap of our professional and personal lives.

Research has shown that the world's mobile worker population will grow to 1.3 billion by 2015 (that's only one year away). Technology further creates a blur between work and life. Personal ambition and commitment may be some of the reasons, but by encouraging employees to stay connected, even when they are not in the office, companies don't make it easier for them to get away and enjoy non- work activities.

A Harvard Business School survey showed that 94 percent of professionals work more than 50 hours a week and nearly half work more than 65 hours per week. Employees can face difficult and exhausting conditions that have adverse effects on them as a result. These effects include burn out, health issues, and an increase in workplace violence. Work-life balance is increasingly becoming impossible to obtain.

A recent Forbes article provided the following tips on how to find the balance that is right for you.

1. Let go of perfectionism. A healthier option is to strive for excellence, not perfectionism.
2. Unplug. Make "quality time" true quality time. Shut your phone off and enjoy the moment. By not reacting to the updates from work, you can develop a stronger habit of resilience.
3. Exercise and meditate. It's important to refresh your mind, body and soul. Do some sort of exercise, yoga or meditation.
4. Limit time-wasting activities and people. Identify what's important in your life and draw boundaries to devote quality time to these high priority people and activities.
5. Change the structure of your life. Take a birds-eye view of your life and ask what changes can make it easier. Then focus on those activities you specialize in and value most.

6. Start small. Build from there. If you're trying to change a certain script in your life, start small and experience some success. Build from there.

Alexander Kjerulf—founder of Woohoo, an international thought leader, and author of topics relating to happiness at work—summed it up nicely when he said, "The ultimate goal is to avoid separating work and life into separate spheres, and find the sweet spot that allows you to do both without neglecting the other."

As leaders, we want to think about what we can do to make the workplace less difficult and more pleasant for our teams. Employees who are able to balance their work, family and life commitments are likely to stay and contribute more to the organization.

So perhaps the title of this article should be: What's important for them and how would you like for them to be?

With Finite Resources and Infinite Needs, Do You Navigate Your Time Wisely?

As individuals move up the leadership ladder, they often find that time becomes a scarce commodity. There is always more to do with little time to do it. We can't do everything ourselves so we have to set priorities in order to manage our time effectively.

One way to manage our time more effectively is to set personal goals. Setting goals is essential for setting priorities. If we set goals, we can determine what is critical to our mission, what is important, and what is nice to get done if we have the time. If we write out a work plan, we can then determine the sequence of events necessary to get the tasks completed.

Determine what your time is worth. By attaching a monetary value to your time, you can then ask yourself, "Is this worth the use of my time?" Review your calendar for the past 90 days and identify your three biggest time wasters. If reviewing your calendar is not effective, then keep track of your activities over the next 90 days and identify your time wasters that way. Once you have done that, set plans to reduce the three biggest time wasters by 50 percent. This could be done by being more effective in your use of emails and voice mails. For example, when making a call, jot down the points you want to cover before you dial the number. Learn to shut down conversations that aren't necessary. Just say, "I have another task I have to get done, can we continue this conversation another time?"

Set deadlines for yourself and use your best time of day for the toughest tasks. If you do your best work in the morning, don't waste that time on less important items.

Delegate time-consuming work to others whenever possible. Effectively delegating things you don't have to do yourself empowers your team and helps them grow. It's also a good way to develop leadership. If you effectively delegate to others, it creates a win-win situation.

If you know other professionals who manage their time well, observe what they do and compare that to what you do. You can adopt their time management practices if they are practices that work for you.

Many times, we don't have time to dwell on our choices, rather we have to make them on the spot, without all the data we would like to have (See previous article on ambiguity). We cannot be right all of the time. We should not try to be a perfectionist or we will miss many opportunities.

Many times, we just have a hard time saying no. Saying no is particularly difficult if you are a Type Two (Helper) Enneagram Personality. People will always ask you to help them, to do something they can't do, putting more on your plate than you have time to do.

Managing your time effectively means having the ability to say no. If someone requesting your help has already asked you to do other things, ask them which of those things they would like to cancel or postpone in order to allow you to accomplish their most recent request. In this way, you get to say yes and no by letting them choose.

Finally, remember that others you interact with may also be under time constraints. Be efficient with their time as well. Get to the point and get it done. Give them the opportunity for new discussions, but if they don't have anything else to add, say "Thanks" and be on your way.

Managing our time is a great leadership competency. To quote Robert Orben, "Time flies. It's up to you to be the navigator."

How Do You Handle Situations When the Solutions Are Ambiguous?

As a manager or leader, we don't always have all the information we need to make critical decisions. In many cases, we face ambiguity. Ambiguity is about doubtfulness, uncertainty, or vagueness. Many times leadership is about not knowing yet making the best of the moment without assurances about what the outcome might be.

Many problems managers and leaders face are ambiguous –neither the problem nor the solution is clear. If we had all the time in the world, and 100 percent of the information, we could make decisions that are more accurate, more often. However, the real reward goes to those who make good decisions most of the time, with few or no precedents regarding how similar problems were solved.

There are several ways we can handle ambiguity. One way is to take small, incremental steps. How we deal with uncertainty depends on how we tolerate errors and mistakes, and how we face any criticism that might follow. We might be able to make a series of smaller decisions, get feedback, make corrections, and move forward a little further. Sometimes the second or third try works best.

Another way to deal with ambiguity is to broaden our horizons. Few people are motivated by uncertainty and chaos. However, many leaders are challenged by solving problems others have not solved, in essence going where no one has gone before. They enjoy learning new things and exploring new horizons. Another process to deal with ambiguity is to get better organized. Set priorities, focus on the critical issues, and let go of the trivia. Learn how to become more effective and efficient in our work processes, and discipline ourselves by developing a set of best practices.

Don't be afraid to fail. We often fail the first time we try something new. Anything worth doing can take repeated effort. We can learn from our mistakes by creating immediate feedback loops. As leaders, we will make many mistakes and have many failures because of the many ambiguities we face. We can't always be sure of success. If we face problems no one else has faced, it's likely no one else knows what to do either. If we make a mistake, we can always ask ourselves what we have learned from it.

Stress will always come into the equation. The more ambiguity, the more stress we will have to manage. When this happens, we can become ungrounded, get frustrated, and many times become upset. It can be a very emotional time. If that happens, let the problem go for a while. Do something else and come back to it after you have a chance to calm down.

Change is about letting go of one thing and reaching for the next. This can be scary, but we have to let go in order to reach out. Many times, it will feel like we are trying to hold onto air until we get to a new place. If we are afraid to fail, we will stay in the same place. We will be safe, but nothing will have changed. We have to let go to change; we have to visualize that next outcome. We have to want it, go after it, or invite it in, experiment with it.

Not everything comes neatly wrapped. We should feel comfortable making mistakes, fixing them, and moving forward. It won't always be perfect.

As Edward de Bono, a British physician, author, inventor and consultant once wrote:

"In the future, instead of striving to be right at a high cost, it will be more appropriate to be flexible and plural at a lower cost. If you cannot accurately predict the future, then you must flexibly be prepared to deal with various possible futures."

Six Easy Steps to Developing A High-Performing Team

There is nothing better than a talented team pulling together in one direction, accomplishing great things for your organization. If you don't have a well-functioning team, you simply have a group of people who work in isolation with no input from other team members, little collaboration, and a loss of opportunities to learn from each other and from their experiences.

While teams may be strange and uncomfortable for many, they are the best way to interact with each other, develop a consensus, and work towards a common goal. In a well-functioning team, each member is aware of what the other team members are working on so that the final deliverable is very cohesive.

It takes time to build a well-functioning team, certainly longer than managing one person at a time. Once you've brought a well-functioning team together, it is easier to build sustained capability to perform and maximize strengths while covering individual weaknesses. In addition, you will have more time to work on other priorities because your team members will be helping each other.

Glenn Llopis, a contributor to Forbes Magazine, wrote an article in October 2012 on ways to build teams to last. He stated that team building is an art and science, and the leader who can build a high-performing team is worth his or her weight in gold.

He mentions six ways successful teams are built to last:

1. **Be Aware of How You Work.** Be your own boss, be flexible, and know who you are as a leader.
2. **Get to Know the Rest of the Team**. Think of your team as puzzle pieces that can be placed together in various ways.
3. **Clearly Define Goals and Responsibilities**. A team should operate as a mosaic whose unique strengths and differences convert into a powerful united force.
4. **Be Proactive with Feedback.** Take the time to remind someone of how and what they can be doing better. Learn from them. Don't complicate the process of constructive feedback. Feedback is two-way communication.
5. **Acknowledge and Reward.** When people are acknowledged, their work brings them greater satisfaction and becomes more purposeful.
6. **Always Celebrate Success.** Celebration is a short-lived activity. Don't ignore it. Take the time to live in the moment, and remember what allowed you to cross the finish line.

Not everyone has the skills to develop great teams. It takes a special kind of leader with a keen understanding of people, knowing their strengths, and doing what it takes to get them excited to work with each other.

As a leader, it is important to allow roles within the team to evolve naturally, delegate and empower others, create a climate of innovation and experimentation, build a sense of joy and fun for the team, and set the standard by modeling it.

Do You Have the Courage to Stand Alone?

Developing our managerial courage is an important leadership quality. Leading isn't always easy; it takes courage to lead people through challenging times. It can encompass making an objective decision and doing what is right under the circumstances. It is a quality we can't always define, though it generally consists of our values, self-awareness, humility, confidence, objectivity, and the willingness to take risks.

Saying what needs to be said at the right time, to the right people, in the right manner takes courage. If the stakes are high, it can be uncomfortable. When we take tough positions and speak out we can stand alone. Standing alone requires self-confidence and a strong sense of self. Leaders often stand alone, which is riskier than following and requires a lot of internal security.

Leadership courage means we must face the truth and express it. Sometimes it means we have the courage to rely on others or to make decisions in risky or uncertain situations. Certainly it means being outside of our comfort zone and pushing our limits. As leaders we have to express courage every day, at every level of our organization. As a leader we are often expected to act with courage.

It doesn't mean we are always right; we are wrong many times, but we learn to accept personal responsibility. When we speak up we often take the heat; others keep it to themselves. When we take the heat; others keep it to themselves. When we take the Heat; we build our heat shield. If we know we're right, standing courageously is well worth the heat. If it turns out we are wrong, we should admit it and move on.

Taking a strong stand takes confidence. We can build that confidence by getting a good scope of the problem, talking to other people, and asking for advice. When we pick an option we should develop the rationale and stand tall until proven wrong. It is also important to consider the opposing view and prepare responses, always expecting pushback.

Keeping your cool is also important. If you have negative emotional reactions, others may think you have problems taking tough positions. Learn to identify negative reactions and control them. You can pause, breathe, or ask a question to buy time. Leadership courage means searching for a better outcome, not destroying others. Even if you are totally right, empathizing with others is important, especially if emotions run high.

We should understand that we will be wrong many times. Most successful managers were promoted to leadership positions because they had the guts to stand alone, not because they were always right. Studies have shown that managers are right 65 percent of the time. Put those errors on your menu because a balanced diet has to have spinach. Don't let the possibility of being wrong hold you back.
Push your envelope, take chances, and suggest bold new ideas. If you fail, treat it as a learning experience. Nothing ventured, nothing gained. Balance your messages and don't put everything in the negative.

You may have to work with the same people again, so do something to show goodwill. Compliment them and help them achieve something so they too have some successes. Balancing the scales will pay dividends in the future.

Standing alone does not always mean going it alone. It means trusting yourself and taking the risk to let yourself be seen, standing firm in your beliefs even when your internal voice challenges you.

Is Being "Lonely at the Top"
A Way of Leadership?

Being personable is a leadership characteristic and strength. It means being able to put others at ease and relate to a variety of people. Being skilled at being approachable means relating well to all kinds of people – up, down, sideways, inside and outside of the organization. It means building constructive and effective relationships. Importantly, it can also mean using diplomacy and tack, which can be beneficial in defusing high-tension situations.

Many managers and leaders see remoteness as a good thing, thinking that "keeping a distance is good," or "I don't want to be warm and fuzzy." In many cases, leaders are aware they aren't "a people person," are not overly concerned because they thought "work was work," or take the position that they are "not here to win a popularity contest." The idea that keeping a healthy distance is good leadership is "old school."

Adopting a segregated style is not healthy. People won't know what to make of it, which can lead to more stress, disengage co-workers, and make them reluctant to approach you with information that may be critical for you to lead. A key to getting along with people is to hold back our personal reactions and focus on others first. It's about working from the outside in.

Managing the first three minutes of a relationship is important. The tone is set and first impressions are formed. It is important we work on being open and approachable—listening, sharing, understanding and comforting.

Being a good listener is also key. It means listening without interrupting, asking clarifying questions, and not instantly judging. It's also about having effective non-verbal communications skills, appearing and sounding relaxed, smiling, being calm, and maintaining good eye contact. When speaking, it's important to keep an open body posture, speak in a paced and pleasant tone, and avoid being forceful or going into too much detail. It's also important to avoid glancing at our watch, fiddling with paperwork, or giving the impression of "I'm busy."

Arrogant people devalue others and their contributions, making them feel diminished, rejected, and upset. To avoid this, read your audience. Learn what people look like when they are uncomfortable with you. Do they cringe? Do they back up? Do they stand outside your door hoping not to be invited in? Make a point of reading others, especially during the first three minutes you engage with them.

Leadership means servicing other people's needs. Being personable may not be the most important aspect of leadership, but it can contribute significantly to your downfall. But know that people can change.

First we have to acknowledge that change is wanted and necessary. Then we must take the necessary actions to become more approachable. The essence of approachability starts with attitude. Being professional and approachable are mutually exclusive.

In many cases being unapproachable can be a blind spot, something coaching can help identify and resolve. Even highly talented individuals can be rendered ineffective if they don't develop their leadership characteristics.

Can You Adjust Your Skills to Meet The Challenges of the Future?

Today's world and work environment is rapidly changing. Skills acquired from past experiences may now be out of date or less useful. They are unlikely to be adequate for the future challenges or opportunities we will face. Fortunately, developing our personal and interpersonal skills is a leadership competency. We can be more successful if we continue to grow and change throughout our career.

Effective leaders learn to constantly adjust; otherwise they can become ineffective and obsolete. One insurance against this is to continually acquire new skills. Preparing for an uncertain future and potential opportunities is a way to get and stay ahead of our competition.

Too many times we want a quick fix. We don't want to put in the time and effort necessary to develop ourselves for future growth. One of the first things we can do to change this is to "know thyself" as the Greek philosopher Socrates once suggested. We have to know our "blind spots." A blind spot is one of the worst things we can have. If we don't know our blind spots, we can go into areas unprepared or ill-prepared. This can result in disaster.

If we can identify our blind spots, we can get to know ourselves. If we know our default settings and motivational core, we can greatly facilitate our growth by being aware of what is most centrally driving our ego agenda. We have to be aware of our personality patterns because in most cases the mechanisms of our personality are invisible to us. If we are able to bring a nonjudgmental awareness to the reactivity of our personality, we can discover a vast part of ourselves and learn how to improve our personal and interpersonal skills.

To learn your personality type and potential blind spots, I recommend the Enneagram assessment. It is a quick way to identify talents, strengths and blind spots. All of my coaching clients and workshop participants to take the assessment before we start working together.

Another development tool is to do a simple skills audit. Poll 10 people who know you well enough to give you detailed feedback on what you do well and not well, what they would like to see you keep doing, start doing and stop doing. Use the results to help you develop skills you need without wasting time on the areas you don't need.

Also, think about what's important in your current job as well as the next two or three jobs you want to strive for. Find successful people in these jobs and ask them what skills they need to use to be successful.

Finally, find others who understand that you take your personal and professional development seriously. State your needs and ask for their help. You will be surprised how many will be willing to assist. They will give the benefit of the doubt and support to those who aren't arrogant, admit their shortcomings, and try to do something about them.

You can also engage the services of a certified, professional coach. Having a coach is a great way to help identify your blind spots and develop your full potential.

Personal development should be a lifelong process. It's a way for us to assess our skills and qualities, consider our aims in life, and set goals in order to realize and maximize our potential.

To quote American Hall of Fame basketball coach John Wooden, "If I am through learning, I am through."

Does a Broken Bone Heal in Isolation? Does an Organization?

A broken bone does not heal in isolation. The recovery process utilizes the whole body, making the healing faster and more complete.

An organization is a living system, which we can compare to a living organism. Within an organization, there are different functions, much like our hands, feet, heart, and lungs. All of these parts working together make it possible for our body to perform. If one part of the body suffers, the whole system suffers.

The same is true of an organization. If one part of the system is underperforming, the whole organization suffers. When the whole system is involved in progressive development, all parts of the organization are improved.

Most people get promoted because of their individual contributions to an organization. In fact, it may be because they were unlike the rest of the members of a team. Sometimes they are held back because other team members held them back from accomplishing things.

However, the best way to accomplish something in most cases is by having a well-functioning, high performing team. Well-functioning teams can out produce the collective efforts of individuals.

So what conditions are necessary to have a well-functioning team? One of the tools we use in our Ascending Leaders Program™ for Team Development measures two areas: Productivity and Engagement.

Productivity strengths support the team in achieving results, accomplishing goals, and staying on course to reach objectives. Seven productivity attributes are necessary to achieve high team performance:

1. **Alignment:** The team has a sense of common mission and purpose.
2. **Goals & Strategies:** The team has clear objectives and alignment on strategies and priorities.
3. **Accountability:** There is clarity of roles and responsibilities. Team members hold each other accountable.
4. **Proactive:** The team embraces change and sees it as vital to the total organization.
5. **Decision Making:** There is a clear and efficient decision making process.
6. **Resources:** Available resources are well managed to meet objectives.
7. **Team Leadership:** The team leader's role is clear and supportive of the team.

Engagement strengths focus on interrelationships between team members. It is the spirit or tone of the team as a system. Seven engagement attributes of a high achieving team are:

1. **Trust:** There is safe environment to speak your mind openly.
2. **Respect:** There is mutual respect and genuine positive regard.
3. **Camaraderie:** There is a strong sense of belonging to the team.
4. **Communication:** Clear and efficient communication is valued over other less direct approaches.

5. **Constructive Interaction:** The team sees conflict as an opportunity for discovery, growth, and creativity.
6. **Values Diversity:** The team is open-minded and values differences in ideas, backgrounds, perspectives, personalities, approaches, and lifestyles.
7. **Optimism:** The team shares an inspiring vision.

A team is not just a collection of individuals; it is a selection of people brought together for a common purpose with identifiable goals, clear roles, and accountability for results.

Every team has its own unique culture that exerts tremendous influence on the team's ability to perform. Every team member wants to be on a great team and contribute their best. The goal of team coaching is to create the conditions to make that happen.

Can You Become the Other Person and Go From There?

Being an effective leader requires many skills. One of the most important is empathy. Empathy is about recognizing emotions in others and putting yourself in another person's shoes. It is a skill that can be developed.

It should not be confused with sympathy. Empathy means being able to understand the needs of others, being aware of their feelings and how it impacts their perception. It doesn't mean you have to agree with how they see things, but that you appreciate what they're going through.

In leadership, empathy matters. It matters because leaders need to put aside their viewpoint and try to see from the other person's point of view. It matters because it validates the other person's perspective. It matters because it requires us to listen—to listen with our ears, our eyes, our instincts, and our heart.

Developing empathic skills improves our people skills. When we develop the capacity to comprehend or experience other's emotions, it reinforces the concept that leadership is all about people, it's all about the relationship. Effective leaders value their followers as individuals and are more tolerant and willing to understand the position and objectivity of others. When we can accept and leverage diversity because of our differences, and not in spite of them, we can be a more effective empathic leader.

Being willing and able to listen with empathy can set you apart as a leader. There are at least three ways we can be more empathic listeners:

1. Make an effort to recognize verbal and nonverbal cues, such as body language, tone and facial expressions.
2. Make an effort to understand the meaning of the message, summarize the points of agreement or disagreement, and assure them you remember what they say.
3. Give appropriate replies, acknowledge them, and clarify any questions you might have.

In an article on empathy in leadership, Ginny Whitelaw, President of the institute for Zen Leadership, wrote that the best coaching advice she ever received was from Tanouye Roshi, a certified Zen master, who told her, "Become the other person and go from there." She wrote, "to become the other person is to feel their emotional state, see through her eyes, think like she thinks, and see how she views us, our proposition, and the situation at hand.

You can start making big things happen, not by controlling, by connecting; not making war on them, but by becoming the people whose interests are served by those big things."

Once you see beyond yourself and your own concerns, you will realize that there is so much more to discover and appreciate beyond your own world.

How Do You Stay Calm in a Stressful Situation?

There is no shortage of things in our lives that cause us to worry. When one of those things disappears, *we* feel good. But soon another thing pops into our mind, and we start stressing about something else. We all have moments when the demands on our life leave us stressed. It not just about stress when we are about to speak in public, there are all sorts of occasions in life when our nerves get the better of us. When this happens, the anxieties we feel –rapid heartbeat, shortness of breath, sweating, and light-headedness– are normal.

Fortunately, there is something we can do about it. We can use a technique called "Centering." You can use Centering to improve focus and manage stress. It will help you keep a clear head when you face a stressful situation. But it's good for everyday situations as well, such a gathering your thoughts before a difficult conversation or when you must deliver bad news.

There are many ways to "center" yourself, but for this newsletter I'll focus on a simple, three step visualization technique.

1. **Step 1: Focus on Your Breathing**. This is a way to help the body relax and restore its basic functioning to steady your breath. Sit or lie somewhere comfortable. Place one hand on your stomach, and breathe in slowly through your nose. Breathe deep into your stomach, using the air you breathe to push your hand while keeping the rest of your body still. Hold your breath for a couple of seconds before exhaling slowly through your mouth.

2. **Step 2: Find Your Center.** Your "physical center of gravity," is about two inches below your navel. Become familiar with it, and remember where it is and what it feels like. It's important to focus your mind on the "center" of your body. Whenever you feel stressed, return to this "center" and remind yourself that you have balance and control. Once at your center, breathe in deeply at least five times. As you concentrate on your center, you should feel your body stabilize. You can do this prior to a difficult discussion or speech and while sitting in a chair or standing, if you don't have the opportunity to lie down and breathe.

3. **Step 3: Redirect Your Energy**. Channel your energy. Choose an image that works for you. Imagine energy flowing to the center of your body. This image can be a ball, or a hot air balloon, whatever works for you. Put all your negative thoughts into the balloon or ball. As you inhale, say to yourself, "I let..." As you exhale, say "...go." Depending on your imagery, imagine tossing it away, such as throwing the ball, or watching the hot air balloon float away. Let go of whatever is stressing you. Imagine your center filled with calm.

At the next inhalation think about what you want to achieve and focus on it, thinking positively. Use affirmations like "I breathe in calmness and breathe out nervousness," "I trust my inner wisdom and intuition," or "I draw from my inner strength." Or you can repeat a word to yourself, such as "success" or "confidence."

For each self-defeating thought that pops up, such as,

"I'll never get it all done," visualize a large, red stop sign in your mind and think, "Stop." Try to drop the rest of the thought. This takes practice because those thoughts have a lot of "psychic inertia," and that's why we may need a "Stop Sign." Use it liberally.

When you can center yourself in times of distress you will find that you work more efficiently, relate to others more easily, and improve your physical health. You can employ the above techniques anywhere and anytime, in just a minute or two. You can master stress instead of it mastering you.

How Do You Manage Change Successfully?

Change is all around us. Sometimes it is so subtle we hardly notice it. Other times it is so dramatic and sudden that we develop negative and resistant reactions. By nature, we tend to resent and resist change strongly.

The process of change, at any level, can be distressing and create negative emotions or reactions. If change is not handled correctly, it has the potential to cause failures, loss of production, and low morale. In the most dramatic cases, we could lose our most valued employees.

So who is responsible for ensuring that the change process is addressed so that individuals accept change and reduce its impact to manageable levels?

Employees affected by change have the responsibility to continue to do their best work as they experience the different stages of change including denial, anger, dejection, acceptance, and learning and development. An individual's degree of resistance to change is determined by how they perceive the change, good or bad, and how severe they expect the impact on them to be.
The responsibility to manage change is with management and leadership. Change has to be understood and managed so that everyone impacted can cope effectively.

To get the employees to acceptance and learning requires skills on managing change. The key to implementing the change successfully is to communicate what is changing and why. It's important that people understand what is changing, when the change will take place, and why the change is being made. Equally important is to communicate what is not changing.

In order to develop a strategy to manage the change, you must make an effort to understand the reluctance that comes with the change and the need to understand the fears associated with it.

John P. Kotter, a leadership expert and author of *Leading Change*, created the Eight-Stage Change Process of Creating Major Change:

1. Establishing a Sense of Urgency – Inspire people to move, make objectives real and relevant.
2. Creating the Guiding Coalition – Get the right people in place with the right emotional commitment, and the right mix of skill levels.
3. Developing a Vision and Strategy – Get the team to establish a simple vision and strategy, focus on emotional and creative aspects necessary to drive service and efficiency.
4. Communicating the Change Vision – Involve as many people as possible, communicate the essentials, appeal to people's needs. De-clutter communications.
5. Empowering Broad-Based Action – Remove obstacles, enable constructive feedback and support from leaders.
6. Generating Short-Term Wins – Aim for achievable wins and recognize those who made the wins possible.
7. Consolidating Gains and Producing More Change – Foster and encourage determination and persistence, encourage ongoing progress. Highlight achievements and future milestones.

8. Anchoring New Approaches in the Culture –
   Reinforce the value of successful change via
   recruitment, promotion, and new change
   leaders. Weave change into the culture.

The first four steps help defrost the status quo. Steps five to seven introduce new practices. Step eight grounds the changes in the organizations' culture, helping them stick.

What's important for change leaders is to manage the issue. Don't try to rationalize things or waste time wishing people were more predictable. Instead focus on maintaining clear communication channels so you understand what is coming and what it means to them.

How Can You Use Your Three Brains to Lead?

In a previous article series about the Enneagram (February – October 2013) I wrote about the nine Enneagram personalities. Each type functions in one of the three basic components of the human psyche: instinct, feeling, or thinking. No matter what type of personality we are, our personality contains the three components. All three interact with each other, and we cannot work on one without affecting the others.

In their book *The Wisdom of the Enneagram*, Don Richard Riso and Russ Hudson remind us that in Enneagram theory, these three functions are related to Centers in the human body, and the personality fixation is associated primarily in one of these centers. Types Eight, Nine, and One comprise the Instinctive (Gut) Triad; types Two, Three, and Four comprise the Feeling (Heart) Triad; and types Five, Six, and Seven are in the Thinking (Head) Triad.

Which of the three types, or which of the three brains, do you use to lead?

There was an excellent article by Vikki Brock, EMBA, PCD, MCC in *Choice* magazine Volume 12 Number 4, pages 33-35 titled **The Triad, How are our three brains impacted by coaching**. Following are key concepts excerpted from her article.

"Scientific research has shown we have three brains – the one in our head, the one in our heart, and the one in our gut. These three brains have control over the decisions we make. Aristotle, in his masterpiece Rhetoric, defines three ways to persuade an audience: Logos (an appeal to logic or head brain), pathos (an appeal to emotion or heart brain), and ethos (credibility of the speaker or gut brain).

In the *Wizard of Oz*, three main characters in the book were the Scarecrow, who was looking for a brain; the Tin Woodsman who wanted a heart; and the Cowardly Lion who wanted courage – or head, heart, and guts. This same triad is apparent when we reflect on what people say: trust your gut...listen to your heart...use your head.

Each brain has core competencies. When we use the **Gut Brain** we rely on our gut often for quick decision-making; that fight or flight response. When using the **Heart Brain**, we use it mostly for processing emotions (joy, anger, hate, love, empathy). It helps you discover what is important to you in life. And the **Head Brain** is primarily used to reason, to analyze and to synthesize information. Alignment of these three brains creates a "flow" state where each brain is functioning at its efficient best.

"When an individual makes a decision or responds to a situation from only one brain and ignores the others, it affects his or her decision-making. If they use the **Gut Brain**, they will likely be reactive, impulsive, and action oriented. This can be useful when safety or survival is threatened. If they use the **Heart Brain**, they will be concerned about self-image, impact on others, and lives of others. When the **Head Brain** is used, they plan and prepare and focus on what could go wrong."

"If you over rely on one or two of your brains, practice and integrate trusting your gut, listening to your heart, and using your head."

"When you are faced with making a decision or responding to a situation from one brain and ignoring the others, ask yourself the following questions: What does your gut tell you? What does your heart feel? What does your head say?"

Does Practicing Gratitude Make You a Better Leader?

An important aspect of leadership is gratitude, or showing gratitude for who people are and what they do. Expressing your gratitude connotes a positive emotion or attitude that recognizes something you have received by acknowledging those who have helped you achieve it.

People who are not grateful tend to be less generous. They are centered on what they deserve or how they have been short-changed. They tend to have a "hoard it" mentality, and cling to what they have.

Leadership entails building community, and expressing gratitude can build healthier communities while deepening the culture of gratitude within an organization. It is one way leaders can walk their talk, and embodies a culture of gratitude in an organization. Think about people who have helped you get where you are. I'm sure you feel grateful for what they have done to help you. Why not show that gratitude?

Expressing your gratitude to those who have helped you gives them a sense of self-worth, which triggers other helpful behaviors. The Return on Investment (ROI) on a simple "thank-you" goes a long way – probably much further than we might think. Taking the opportunity to express gratitude is, without a doubt, a cost-free opportunity to motivate.

Developing a gratitude mindset is important in developing the leadership practice of gratitude. This can be difficult in the frenzied work environment many of us are in. Like most things that are worth developing, it takes practice to develop that mindset until it becomes a habit.

Consider these simple practices you can use to start to develop a gratitude mindset:

1. Keep a gratitude journal. Journaling is a great way to develop mindsets and neural pathways to notice the positive. Simply keep a journal every day about what you are grateful for. It will boost your positivity and energy.
2. Notice the contributions that others make. In interactions with others, make it a practice to look for one area of strength or contribution they make. Don't set the standard too high, simply catch them doing something right.
3. Create a culture of gratitude. One simple way to do this is to give everyone note cards they can hand out to others as often and as freely as they want. The note cards can say: "Thanks for making a difference." Individuals may want to expand the note to explain what it was that person did to warrant the gratitude note.
4. Begin your day by expressing your gratitude to three people, then get to work. End your day with an act of gratitude, then go home.

Leadership is about creating community. It's about the values, goals and determinations we share. These communities go by different names; most commonly, we call them teams, companies, crews, departments, divisions or organizations. But the one thing they all have in common is that their effectiveness is directly related to how we create that feeling of one-ness, that sense of camaraderie.

Pick your own activity to develop a gratitude culture. I am sure you can come up with one or two of your own. Just start practicing it.

Do You Give Your Employees a
Reason to Be Engaged?

Wikipedia defines an engaged employee as one who is fully involved in and enthusiastic about their work, and thus will act in a way that furthers their organization's interest.

According to an employee engagement report by Scarlet Surveys, only 31 percent of employees are actively engaged in their jobs.

If employee engagement is so important, then why are organizations so ineffective at it? And what is your responsibility as a leader in an organization to create an environment that is conducive to employees making good business choices?

Research has shown there are correlations between employee engagement and desirable business outcomes such as retention of talent, customer service, individual and team performance, and business productivity.

Employee engagement should not be an occasional effort, but a yearlong key strategic initiative that should drive employee performance and continuous improvement.

One reason organizations don't employ an effective strategy is because it is not easy work — they cannot immediately see it in their bottom line. Another is that many organizations don't make the commitment of time, tools, attention, and training. When measured effectively, one can see the relationship and correlation between specific positive business outcomes and positive employee engagement.

Organizations can take steps to develop a culture of employee engagement if they understand the role of leadership in communicating, developing, and rewarding employees. An article by Patricia Lotich, in *The Thriving Business*, identified at least ten ways an organization can create an employee engagement culture. Here is a summary of them:

1. **Strong Vision**. Develop a defined and well-communicated vision.
2. **Consistent Communication**. Communicate how the organization is doing, how goals are being accomplished, and how employees contribute to achieving the organization's objectives.
3. **Supervision Interaction.** Direct supervisors should demonstrate their care for employees as individuals.
4. **Employee Development.** Employees should be given the opportunity to develop and grow professionally.
5. **Team Environment.** Developing a strong team environment can help foster engaged employees.
6. **Culture of Trust.** Employees need to trust each other as well as their leadership.
7. **Clear Expectations.** Employees need to know what is expected of them.
8. **Reward and Recognition.** Employees need to feel validated and acknowledged as part of the organization.
9. **Employee Satisfaction.** Employees need to feel like they are part of the process.
10. **Competitive Pay and Benefits.** While not a key indicator, offering competitive pay, benefits,

and reasonable working conditions is a strategy for strong employee engagement.

Having effective engagement practices and understanding what is meaningful to employees can get you to work towards a more motivated and high-performing workforce. Commitment to an intentional culture of employee engagement is important for employees to thrive and for retaining the top performers. The bottom line is engaged employees are good for business.
Let me close with two quotes about why employee engagement is so important:

"When people go to work, they shouldn't
have to leave their hearts at home."
–Betty Bender

"Employee engagement is an investment we make for the privilege of future proofing our organization's productivity and performance."
– Ian Hutchinson, Chief Engagement Officer, Life by Design

Avoiding Responsibility is Like Throwing People under the Bus

Companies are run by people, and people often hate taking responsibility for their own actions. All too often, the inclination is to blame someone or something else to bolster a self-image and explain away a problem.

In today's political culture of spin, modern leaders are less ready than ever to admit fallibility. The phrase 'mistakes were made …' has entered the political lexicon as the most passive and detached way of acknowledging error rather than accepting responsibility.

As a leader, you're responsible for what happens in your organization. You need to question the decisions and processes that hold your organization together because you'll be held accountable, and the consequences can be severe.

Responsibility is not about power, but power brings about greater responsibility, and the executive or manager who doesn't acknowledge their responsibility can indeed be a poor leader. When you accept a position of leadership, you accept the responsibility that comes with it. It is not an acceptance that should be taken lightly.

As a responsible leader, your main focus should be to ensure that you and your organization act responsibly, ethically and fairly. More people are needed in influential positions who embrace ideas around responsible leadership.

Gandhi claimed that, "If we could change ourselves, the tendencies in the world would also change." So it starts with us. It's not easy; there can be many obstacles, particularly if you're fighting the status quo. We can begin by asking – what counts as great leadership in responsible organizations?

Taking responsibility is the right thing to do. When you constantly blame others and view yourself as a victim, you surround yourself with anger, resentment and negative thoughts. This process can bring on chronic stress.

So quit playing the blame game and take some time alone to review the situation. Admit when you might have helped create the problem, look for a lesson to be learned, and then take the initiative to learn from it.

The last thing you want is a reputation of throwing people under the bus. It may help if you take the time to step back and avoid knee-jerk responses. Make sure you give credit when credit is due, as this is important as well.

Why Your Leadership Style May Not Be Effective

We are generally prone to get comfortable in using one leadership style for most situations. While it's important to recognize which style we feel more comfortable with, that particular style may not serve us well all the time. What's important to understand is that our style may not be effective at that given time, or for the situation we are facing.

When people ask me which leadership style is best, I tell them "It depends." It depends on the situation and the people you are leading. It depends on the degree of control you feel you need to have over the people you're leading. It depends on how much independence and freedom your team is prepared to handle. It depends on how much trust you have in the people you lead.

We typically have a way of leading that becomes our natural style, or one we prefer or gravitate to in a crisis. What's important is to become familiar with different leadership styles and apply the one that works at a given time, in a given situation, for a specific team, or for specific persons.

Leadership, like leaders, comes in many different styles. A landmark 2000 Harvard Business Review study conducted by Daniel Goleman uncovered six specific leadership behaviors. It also determined their effect on the corporate culture and each style's effect on bottom-line profitability.

In summary, below are the six leadership styles Coleman uncovered during the three-year study with over 3000 middle-level managers.

1. **The coercive leader** demands immediate compliance. If this style were summed up in one phrase, it would be "Do what I tell you." The coercive style is most effective in times of crisis. This style can also help control a problem teammate when everything else has failed. However, it should be avoided in almost every other case because it can alienate people and stifle flexibility and inventiveness. This style is the least effective.

2. **The authoritative leader** mobilizes the team toward a common vision and focuses on end goals, leaving the means up to each individual. If this style were summed up in one phrase, it would be "Come with me." The authoritative style works best when the team needs a new vision or explicit guidance is not required. This style is the most effective.

3. **The affiliative leader** works to create emotional bonds that bring a feeling of belonging to the organization. If this style were summed up in one phrase, it would be "People come first." The affiliative style works best in times of stress, when teammates need to heal from a trauma, or need to rebuild trust. This style should not be used exclusively because a sole reliance on praise and nurturing can foster mediocre performance and a lack of direction.

4. **The democratic leader** builds consensus through participation. If this style were summed up in one phrase, it would be "What do you think?" The democratic style is most effective when the leader needs the team to buy into or

have ownership of a decision, plan, or goal, or is uncertain and needs fresh ideas from qualified teammates. It is not the best choice in an emergency situation or when teammates are not informed enough to offer sufficient guidance to the leader.

5. **The coaching leader** develops people for the future. If this style were summed up in one phrase, it would be "Try this." The coaching style works best when the leader wants to help teammates build lasting personal strengths that make them more successful overall. It is least effective when teammates are defiant and unwilling to change or learn.

6. **The pacesetting leader** expects and models excellence and self-direction. If this style were summed up in one phrase, it would be "Do as I do, now." The pacesetting style works best when the team is already motivated and skilled, and the leader needs quick results. This style should be used sparingly.

If you master four or more of these leadership approaches– especially the authoritative, democratic, affiliative, and coaching styles – you'll have the best climate and business performance. The most effective leaders match their style to fit the situation.

www.ingramcontent.com/pod-product-compliance
Lightning Source LLC
Chambersburg PA
CBHW070942210326
41520CB00021B/7019